Snap books®

Robert Pattinson

by Jennifer M. Besel

Capstone press®

Mankato, Minnesota

Snap Books are published by Capstone Press,
151 Good Counsel Drive, P.O. Box 669, Mankato, Minnesota 56002.
www.capstonepress.com

Books published by Capstone Press are manufactured with paper
containing at least 10 percent post-consumer waste.

Library of Congress Cataloging-in-Publication Data
Besel, Jennifer M.
    Robert Pattinson / by Jennifer M. Besel.
    p. cm. — (Snap books. Star biographies)
    Includes bibliographical references and index.
    Summary: "Describes the life and career of Robert Pattinson" — Provided by publisher.
    ISBN 978-1-4296-3729-9 (library binding)
    1. Pattinson, Robert, 1986– — Juvenile literature. 2. Actors Juvenile literature. — United States — Biography.
I. Title. II. Series.
PN2287.P277B37 2010
792.0'28092 — dc22   2009002748

Editor: Megan Peterson
Designer: Juliette Peters
Media Researcher: Marcie Spence

Photo Credits:
Alamy/Allstar Picture Library, 18; AP Images/Chris Pizzello, 27; AP Images/Paul Drinkwater/NBCU Photo Bank, 29; AP Images/Tammie Arroyo, 7; Corbis/Steven Georges/Press-Telegram, 25; Courtesy of How To Films Ltd., 13; Courtesy of Tower House Preparatory School, 10; Getty Images Inc./Franco S. Origlia, 21; Getty Images Inc./Jon Furniss/WireImage, cover; Getty Images Inc./Kevin Winter, 6; Getty Images Inc./Lester Cohen/WireImage, 5; Newscom, 16; Newscom/Murray Close/Warner Bros. Pictures, 17; Newscom/Summit Entertainment/MCT, 23; Supplied by Capital Pictures/Steve Finn, 9; Tandem Productions/VIP Medienfonds 2&3 Courtesy of Sony Pictures Home Entertainment, 15

Essential content terms are **bold** and are defined at the bottom of the page where they first appear.

Table of Contents

CHAPTER 1

Fan Frenzy

Cameras flashed. Reporters shouted questions. And fans went crazy. It was November 17, 2008, the night of the much-anticipated premiere of the movie *Twilight*. More than 600 screaming fans crowded around the red carpet. Hundreds more spilled out across the street. Holding homemade signs and wearing *Twilight* T-shirts, fans chanted for their favorite actors. Taylor Lautner, who played Jacob Black, took pictures with fans. Cam Gigandet, James in the movie, slapped hands down the rows of people. The film's leading lady, Kristen Stewart, quietly signed autographs and posed for photographers.

Then came Robert Pattinson, who played the lead role of Edward Cullen. The crowed erupted into a chorus of screaming and crying. Robert, who usually goes by Rob, looked sharp in a fitted black suit and tie. He signed everything from books to pizza boxes. He stopped for interviews with reporters from around the world. But the noise outside the Mann Village Theater in Los Angeles was deafening. Rob had to shout his answers.

premiere — the first public showing of a film

Rob had trouble hearing over the screaming fans at the *Twilight* premiere.

"This is my life. People know my name and ambush me in public and try to figure out what hotel I'm staying at and ask me to bite them and want to touch my hair. I have accepted it as real now, but it still feels surreal."

— Rob at the *Twilight* premiere, from an interview with *Entertainment Weekly*.

The cast had gathered in Los Angeles for the first screening of the movie *Twilight*. For many in the cast, it would be the first time they would see the finished product. But the intense crowd response almost overshadowed the movie. The screening was delayed 45 minutes so Rob and his costars could greet more fans.

After the screening, the cast was ready to celebrate. At the Armand Hammer Museum, the celebs were treated to a fancy party in an outdoor courtyard. Rob and his costars celebrated with chocolate chip cookies on lollipop sticks. Long into the night, fans screamed their love for Rob. For him, the overwhelming response from the fans was unreal. It was a far cry from his **rebellious** childhood in London.

Rob and *Twilight* costar Kristen Stewart posed for photographers at the premiere.

rebellious — struggling against the people in charge

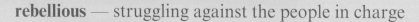

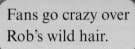

Fans go crazy over Rob's wild hair.

Hairy Headlines

Fans don't just go crazy over Rob's good looks and talents. They also rave about his hair. Rob's hair, a mass of gelled spikes and waves, is his trademark look. On the red carpet, he scrunches up his hair in a kind of nervous habit.

Blogs buzz about Rob's hair and whether or not he washes it. Fans reach out to touch it. His style has become a **phenomenon** of its own. And when he wears his favorite black ski cap, the fans scream for him to take it off. There's so much hype, Rob has even joked about starting his own line of hairstyling products.

Rob created quite a stir in December 2008 when he did the unthinkable — he cut off his signature locks! Online polls quickly confirmed that Rob's heartthrob status was not at risk. Short or long, Rob's hair will always be in the spotlight.

"People are scared of my hair. But it starts washing itself after about three weeks. I'm just saying that. But, yeah, if it doesn't look dirty, why wash it?"
— Rob talks about his famous hair in an interview with *USA Today*.

phenomenon — something unusual or remarkable

CHAPTER 2

Life in London

Robert Thomas Pattinson was born May 13, 1986. He grew up in suburban London, England, the youngest of Richard and Clare Pattinson's three children. Rob's dad sold vintage cars. His mom worked for a modeling agency. Rob's two older sisters, Elizabeth and Victoria, liked to tease him. They even went so far as to dress Rob like a girl and call him Claudia! For fun Rob watched cartoons like *Sharkey & George* and *Hammertime*, featuring rapper MC Hammer. To earn spending money, Rob delivered newspapers.

When he was younger, Rob enjoyed playing music and acting in school plays.

Until age 12, Rob attended London's Tower House Preparatory School.

No Teacher's Pet

Rob was a troublemaker when it came to school. As a young boy, Rob attended the Tower House Preparatory School in London. Rob never did his homework and refused to try hard during class. He was once a lunch monitor. But instead of enforcing the rules, he stole his classmates' french fries. And he even won the "untidy desk award." At age 12, Rob was expelled from school. But he's refused to say what caused the trouble.

At age 13, Rob began attending the Harrodian School in London. At the Harrodian School, drama was a major focus of student life. Rob also got to enjoy the heated outdoor swimming pool, state-of-the-art science labs, and music center.

Two Loves

Rob wasn't big on doing schoolwork. But there were two things that he did work hard at — music and drama. Rob, a devoted musician, developed an interest in music early in his life. He started playing the piano at age 4. When he was 5, he took up the guitar. By age 14, he was fronting a rap trio. His hero was rapper Eminem.

Drama was an activity that Rob enjoyed at school. He acted in several school plays, including *Lord of the Flies*. But acting professionally wasn't really something he'd ever thought about. He really dreamed of being a musician.

Reluctant Star

Rob resisted becoming an actor. But Rob's father watched him in school plays. He saw that his son had a special talent. He wanted Rob to be an actor, and he was very vocal about it. Rob's father encouraged him to join the acting group that worked near their house. Rob refused. But his father kept pushing. Rob went to work at the Barnes Theatre Company at age 15. He helped organize props and move sets.

After the first show he worked on, Rob decided to give acting a try. He **auditioned** for a role in the musical *Guys and Dolls*. To his surprise, he landed the role of a Cuban dancer. Rob found himself becoming a regular in the Barnes Theatre Group. He grabbed the roles of George Gibbs in *Our Town* and Lord Evelyn Oakleigh in *Anything Goes*. After Rob's performance as Alec in *Tess of the d'Urbervilles*, an acting **agent** approached him. The agent convinced Rob to begin an acting career.

"I play a lot of music. That's what I wanted to do before the acting thing accidentally took off — be a musician."
— Rob from an interview with *Vanity Fair*.

audition — to try out for a role

agent — someone who helps actors find work

Rob has been able to use his musical talents in some of his films.

Musically Speaking

Music is a big part of Rob's life. Since his rap trio days, Rob has continued to play music and sing. In school he formed the band Bad Girls with his friends.

Now Rob plays gigs from time to time with three friends. But they aren't a professional band. The guys aren't looking for a record deal. They play their rocky-blues style of music for their own fun and enjoyment. Along with his friends, Rob also writes original music. Two of their songs, "Never Think" and "Let Me Sign," are featured on the *Twilight* soundtrack.

Once in a while, Rob graces open mic nights at clubs. When he plays solo, Rob actually goes by a different name. On stage he becomes Bobby Dupea. Bobby Dupea is a character Jack Nicholson played in the movie *Five Easy Pieces*. And Nicholson is Rob's favorite actor.

Bitten by the Acting Bug

Acting at the Barnes Theatre Company opened many doors for Rob. By age 17, he quickly made the leap from stage to screen. Rob played the role of Giselher in the epic adventure *Ring of the Nibelungs*. The made-for-TV movie gave Rob his first taste of working in front of a camera. Rob lived in his own apartment for three months while filming in Cape Town, South Africa.

Next Rob was cast in a minor role in his first big film, *Vanity Fair*. He even got the chance to work with celeb Reese Witherspoon. In September 2004, Rob was proud to attend the movie's red-carpet premiere. But then came disappointment. As he watched the film for the first time, he realized his scenes had been cut. And no one had even told him.

Rob rebounded with a role in *The Woman Before* at London's Royal Court Theatre. But just one week before opening night, Rob was fired from the play. He learned that an actor's luck could change quickly.

At age 17, Rob (far left) starred in the TV movie *Ring of the Nibelungs*.

Rob had fun filming scenes with Harry Potter costar Daniel Radcliffe.

Becoming a Star

Disappointment didn't last long for Rob. The casting agent from *Vanity Fair* invited Rob to try out for the fourth Harry Potter movie. He was offered the role of quidditch player Cedric Diggory after only two auditions. Rob filmed the action-packed movie for 11 months in England. In one scene, Cedric and Harry chased each other through a maze of hedges. Rob enjoyed performing those stunts with costar Daniel Radcliffe. He didn't even mind the bruises left by the motorized hedges. Rob also spent three weeks learning how to scuba dive for the role.

While on the set, Rob carried a journal and wrote about his experiences on set. He also wrote about his fear of never landing another part.

In November 2005, *Harry Potter and the Goblet of Fire* opened to excited audiences worldwide. Playing Cedric Diggory was a huge boost for Rob's acting career. Movie reviews praised his performance. *Teen People* called him the next Jude Law. The *Times Online* chose him for the British Star of Tomorrow award.

While filming, Rob performed many of his own stunts.

Rob was both excited and nervous to attend the London premiere of *Harry Potter and the Goblet of Fire.*

New Opportunities

Rob's success in the Harry Potter film and his newfound stardom led to many choice roles. He landed lead roles in two made-for-TV movies, *The Haunted Airman* and *The Bad Mother's Handbook*. He also appeared briefly in a flashback scene in the 2007 film *Harry Potter and the Order of the Phoenix*.

The year 2008 would be the best year yet for the young actor. Rob tapped into his comedic side in the United Kingdom movie *How to Be*. In the film he played Art, a 20-year-old man who ends up moving back home. With the assistance of a self-help guide, Art explores his life. Rob's performance earned him the Best Actor Award at the 2008 Strasbourg International Film Festival in Strasbourg, France. Rob also took on the part of legendary artist Salvador Dali in the movie *Little Ashes*. To prepare for the role, he read every biography of Dali he could find. *Little Ashes* premiered at London's Raindance Film Festival in October 2008. But both movies were overshadowed by the role that made Robert Pattinson a household name.

"Harry Potter was what made me become an actor. I credit Harry Potter with everything else that's come since for me."
— Rob from an interview with *MTV*.

The Role of a Lifetime

The book *Twilight* by Stephenie Meyer became a worldwide hit. Teenage girls were crazy over Meyer's painfully beautiful vampire named Edward Cullen. When Summit Entertainment decided to bring *Twilight* to the big screen, fans demanded director Catherine Hardwicke get the casting right.

Hardwicke almost passed up Rob for the part. She had seen a photo of him, but she wasn't impressed. Not really believing he could get the role, Rob flew to California to meet with the director. At Hardwicke's home, he auditioned for the part of Edward. Rob performed a love scene with Kristen Stewart, who had been cast to play Edward's love. That night Hardwicke saw in Robert what she couldn't see in his photo. She had found the actor who could pull off the intense vampire character from Meyer's book.

Rob and Kristen Stewart posed for this promotional photo in Rome, Italy. They traveled the world to promote *Twilight*.

"I did a thing yesterday where I got out of the car, and the whole street ran forward. I was just thinking, like wow. This must have been what it felt like to have a medieval battle."

— Rob from an interview with *Entertainment Weekly*.

Becoming a Vampire

Rob took the role of Edward seriously. He prepared for the part in ways he'd never had to before. For two months, Rob lived alone outside Portland, Oregon, where the cast would film the movie. To explore the **isolation** a vampire might feel, he didn't talk to anyone. Rob wrote journal articles from Edward's point of view. He worked out and ran every day to get in shape. He read and studied everything he could to connect with his character, including Meyer's book. Rob also had to develop an American accent. In his other roles, Rob's natural British accent had worked fine. He'd never done an American drawl before. He watched movies featuring actors James Dean and John Wayne. He studied their pronunciation and tried to copy the way they spoke.

"I tried to make it [Edward] into a real character, rather than just Dracula. A lot of the way Stephenie [Meyer] had written the books was trying to take vampires out of the world of cliché."
— Rob from an interview with *MTV.*

isolation — the condition of being alone

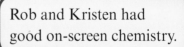
Rob and Kristen had good on-screen chemistry.

Lights, Camera, Action

Filming the movie was a mix of fun and frustration for the actors and crew. Rob arrived on set for makeup at 5:45 each morning. Makeup artists turned his skin pale and styled his hair. Rob put in gold colored contact lenses. Then for many of the scenes, Rob and company had to be rigged on wires. They soared through the air, fighting each other or jumping through treetops. It wasn't easy keeping their balance.

Fighting the weather became a daily task for the cast and crew. Oregon's weather seemed to change by the minute. It would rain, hail, and snow in a single day. The actors huddled in their warm coats between scenes. Then other days the sun would shine — a bad thing when many of the film's characters don't go out in the sun. But through it all, Rob and his costars found plenty to laugh about. They grew to be good friends. And they all worked hard to make the best movie they possibly could.

All the hard work and preparation paid off. When *Twilight* was released in November 2008, reviews raved about Rob's portrayal of Edward. Teens and adults alike flocked to theaters to see Rob play the world's newest vampire. The movie grossed $35.7 million on opening day alone. People calling themselves "fanpires" swarmed Rob in every city and in every country he visited. He had become a true international celebrity.

Twilight was one of the best-selling books of 2008.

From Books to Movies

Acting in *Harry Potter and the Goblet of Fire* and *Twilight* made Rob a superstar. While the roles he played are very different, the movies do have one thing in common. They are both based on best-selling books. And Rob is the only actor to star in both series.

When Rob was first cast as Edward in *Twilight*, fans were furious. Message boards filled with chatter. They said the actor who played Cedric Diggory was not right for the part of Edward Cullen. People posted YouTube videos bashing Catherine Hardwicke's casting decision. About 75,000 fans signed a petition demanding that Edward be recast.

But things turned around when producers released the movie trailer for *Twilight*. All of a sudden, the message boards praised Rob in the role of Edward. *Twilight* fans gushed about the actor they once rejected. And the **mania** surrounding Rob grew to a frenzy.

mania — great enthusiasm

CHAPTER 5

A Breakout Star

After the success of *Twilight*, Rob became one of Hollywood's bright new stars. Fans can't get enough of him. Hollywood moviemakers want him in their films. The magazine *Entertainment Weekly* named him one of the 10 Breakout Stars of 2008. And the Hollywood Film Festival chose Rob for the New Hollywood Award. He's come a long way from the troublesome schoolboy in London.

Even with all the attention, Rob lives a fairly laid-back life. He buys vintage clothing. He drove a 1989 black BMW convertible that cost $2,000 until it died. Now he rents an Audi S4. He also rents his Los Angeles apartment. Instead of eating gourmet meals, Rob keeps his kitchen stocked with peach Snapple and pepperoni Hot Pockets. He gets homesick for London and misses his dog, a white terrier named Patty.

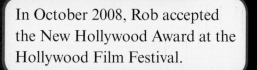

In October 2008, Rob accepted
the New Hollywood Award at the
Hollywood Film Festival.

Never Alone

Rob tries to keep cool about his fame. But fame doesn't provide much privacy or time for rest. **Paparazzi** follow Rob wherever he goes. Magazines pay top dollar for pictures of this rising A-lister. Photographers wait outside his London home and his Los Angeles apartment.

Bodyguards also accompany Rob wherever he goes. Fans are usually nice. But stars like Rob need protection in case fans get a bit too excited. And once in a while, fans might not be happy about something an actor does. Bodyguards help keep Rob out of harm's way.

Perks of Stardom

Being a huge celebrity does come with some perks. Rob is known all around the world. Restaurants and clubs give him prime seating. He gets to wear the latest fashions given to him from well-known designers. He does interviews with other Hollywood celebs like Tyra Banks and Jay Leno. And don't forget about the money. Rob was paid $2 million dollars for his performance in *Twilight*. And sources say he'll get $12 million to play the vampire in the sequel, *New Moon*.

paparazzi — aggressive photographers who take pictures of celebrities for sale to magazines or newspapers

More to Come

Riding his wave of success, Rob already has new projects in the works. Summit Entertainment announced it was moving forward with the second and third movies in the *Twilight* series, *New Moon* and *Eclipse*. Fans will see Rob on the big screen as Edward Cullen when the movies debut in November 2009 and June 2010. Many news reporters have hinted at Rob putting out a CD of original music. And of course there are always the hairstyling products! No matter the role, Rob has made a spot for himself in Hollywood. And fans are sure he'll keep surprising them with his many talents.

Meeting *The Tonight Show* host Jay Leno left Rob feeling starstruck.

Glossary

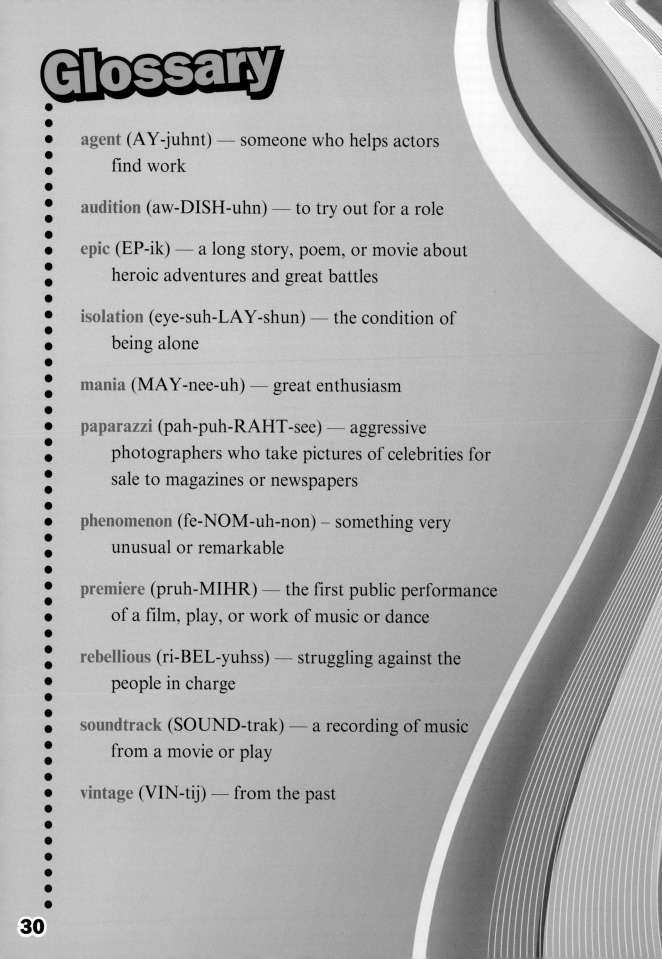

agent (AY-juhnt) — someone who helps actors find work

audition (aw-DISH-uhn) — to try out for a role

epic (EP-ik) — a long story, poem, or movie about heroic adventures and great battles

isolation (eye-suh-LAY-shun) — the condition of being alone

mania (MAY-nee-uh) — great enthusiasm

paparazzi (pah-puh-RAHT-see) — aggressive photographers who take pictures of celebrities for sale to magazines or newspapers

phenomenon (fe-NOM-uh-non) – something very unusual or remarkable

premiere (pruh-MIHR) — the first public performance of a film, play, or work of music or dance

rebellious (ri-BEL-yuhss) — struggling against the people in charge

soundtrack (SOUND-trak) — a recording of music from a movie or play

vintage (VIN-tij) — from the past

Read More

Adams, Isabelle. *Robert Pattinson: Eternally Yours*. New York: Bowen Press, 2008.

Jones, Jen. *Being Famous.* 10 Things You Need to Know About. Mankato, Minn.: Capstone Press, 2008.

Vaz, Mark Cotta. *Twilight: The Complete Illustrated Movie Companion*. New York: Little, Brown and Co., 2008.

Williams, Mel. *Robert Pattinson*. New York: Simon, 2008.

Internet Sites

FactHound offers a safe, fun way to find Internet sites related to this book. All of the sites on FactHound have been researched by our staff.

Here's all you do:

Visit *www.facthound.com*

FactHound will fetch the best sites for you!

Index